FOX PUPS

JEN BESEL

BLACK RABBIT BOOKS

Bolt Jr. is published by Black Rabbit Books
P.O. Box 3263, Mankato, Minnesota, 56002.
www.blackrabbitbooks.com

Michael Sellner, designer; Omay Ayres, photo researcher

Names: Besel, Jennifer M., author.
Title: Fox pups / by Jen Besel.
Description: Mankato, Minnesota : Black Rabbit Books, [2020] | Series: Bolt Jr. baby animals | Includes bibliographical references and index. | Audience: Age 6-8. | Audience: K to Grade 3.
Identifiers: LCCN 2019000750 (print) | LCCN 2019002717 (ebook) | ISBN 9781623101442 (ebook) | ISBN 9781623101381 (library binding) | ISBN 9781644660942 (paperback)
Subjects: LCSH: Foxes—Infancy—Juvenile literature.
Classification: LCC QL737.C22 (ebook) | LCC QL737.C22 B4767 2020 (print) | DDC 599.77513/92—dc23
LC record available at https://lccn.loc.gov/2019000750

Printed in the United States. 5/19

Image Credits

Alamy: Alex Witt, 20–21; Arco Images GmbH, Cover; Arterra Picture Library, 22–23; BIOSPHOTO, 13; iStock: BirdImages, 5; chrisboy2004, 11; IAM-photography, 12; Shutterstock: 4eka, 3, 24; aquatarkus, 7 (cards); Eric Isselee, 4, 10, 21 (inset); Geoffrey Kuchera, 6–7; irishka5, 16–17; Jolanda Aalbers, 1; Neil Burton, 18–19; Richard Peterson, 8–9; yod67, 14–15 (fox)

Contents

CHAPTER 1

A Hungry Baby

A fox pup hides in the grass. It **sneaks** up on its sister. Jump! The pup lands on the other one. Then they wrestle. But soon they need their mother. The pups are hungry!

sneak: to move in a secret way

WEIGHT COMPARISON

newborn pup ◀ ········

about 3 ounces
(85 grams)

Growing Fast

Newborn pups can't see or hear. But they grow quickly. In about two weeks, their eyes and ears open. They can see and hear their fluffy family.

deck of cards
3.4 ounces
(96 grams)

PARTS OF A

Fox Pup

ears
eyes
mouth
paws

CHAPTER 2

Food and Homes

Pups fight and play a lot. They get hungry. At first, they drink their mothers' milk. As they grow, their parents bring them fruit and meat. Pups like fish and small **mammals**.

mammal: an animal that feeds milk to its young and usually has hair or fur

FACT

There are about 12 kinds of foxes.

A Warm House

Foxes live all around the world. They live in forests and deserts. Some even live in mountains. Pups are born in **dens** dug into the ground. They are warm homes for pups.

den: the home of some kinds of wild animals

Where Foxes Live

Europe
Asia
Africa
Australia

CHAPTER 3

Growing Up

Pups have a lot to learn. They watch their parents hunt. Pups aren't good hunters at first. They must learn to use their eyes, ears, and noses to find food.

FACT

Pups lose baby teeth just like human kids.

Making Their Own Homes

Pups don't stay with their parents forever. They leave when they are about eight months old. They make new homes.

Foxes are fully grown by the time they leave home. They soon have pups of their own.

15

Adult Fox's Weight

about 15 pounds (7 kilograms)

Bonus Facts

Most foxes hunt at night.

Adult red foxes have 42 teeth.

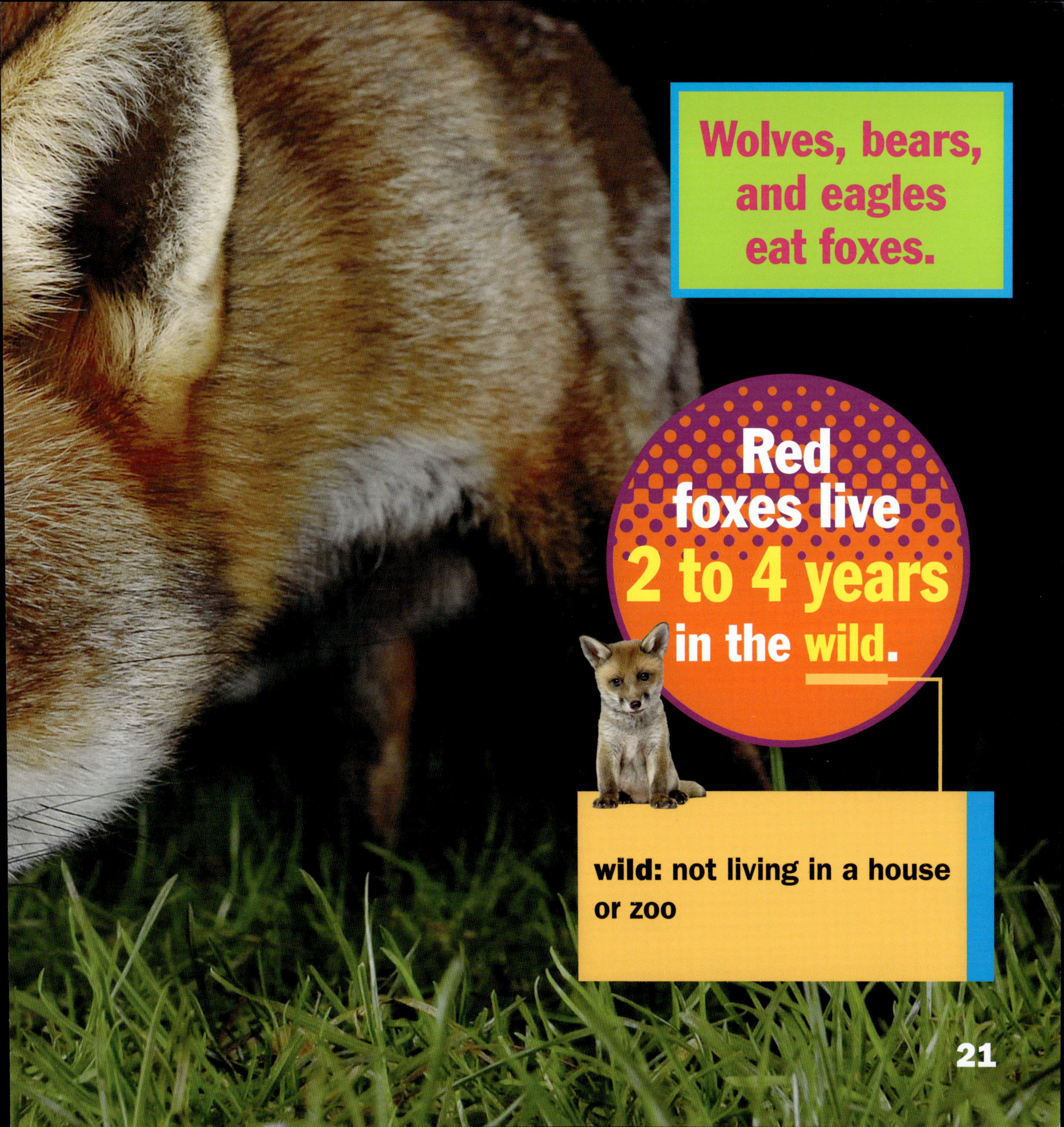

Wolves, bears, and eagles eat foxes.

Red foxes live **2 to 4 years** in the **wild**.

wild: not living in a house or zoo

READ MORE/WEBSITES

Borgert-Spaniol, Megan. *Baby Foxes.* Super Cute! Minneapolis: Bellwether Media, 2016.

Graegin, Stephanie. *Little Fox in the Forest*. New York: Schwartz & Wade Books, 2017.

Nilsen, Genevieve. *Fox Kits*. Forest Babies. Minneapolis: Tadpole Books, 2019.

Arctic Fox
defenders.org/arctic-fox/basic-facts

Fennec Fox
animals.sandiegozoo.org/animals/fennec-fox

Red Fox
www.nationalgeographic.com/animals/mammals/r/red-fox/

GLOSSARY

den (DEN)—the home of some kinds of wild animals

mammal (MAH-muhl)—a type of animal that feeds milk to its young and usually has hair or fur

sneak (SNEEK)—to move in a secret way

wild (WIHLD)—not living in a house or zoo

INDEX